You Don't Know Me Like That!

A Testimony of Hidden Strength and Unseen Battles

JEANETTE LONG

Copyright © 2025 JEANETTE LONG

You Don't Know Me Like That: A Testimony of Hidden Strength and Unseen Battles

All scriptures are taken from the KING JAMES VERSION (KJV): KING JAMES VERSION, public domain.

Published in the USA

ISBN: 979-8-218-76773-0

Dedication

To every woman who's ever been misunderstood, mislabeled, or mistaken for less…
This is for you.

To the teenage mother.
To the broken daughter.
To the single mom, doing it scared.
To the sister who's still running but desperately wants to be caught by grace.
This is your reminder that God never stopped calling your name.

And to my son, Quincy —
Thank you for being my why. You are the testimony I hold in my arms and the reason I kept going.

JEANETTE LONG

Table of Contents

Acknowledgments

First, to my Heavenly Father —
You never gave up on me, even when I gave
up on myself. Thank you for chasing me
down, loving me through my rebellion, and
turning my pain into purpose. All glory
belongs to You.

To my mother —
You were my shelter, my strength, my
shield. You covered me when I couldn't
cover myself. Your unconditional love and
quiet strength shaped the woman I am today.

To my son, Quincy —
You are my greatest blessing. Watching you
grow has been the reward of my faith.
Thank you for your patience, your love, and
your smile — it saved me more times than
you know.

To my family and sister-friends —
You prayed for me, pushed me, and
reminded me who I was when I forgot.

Thank you for standing by me when life didn't make sense.

To every woman who ever walked through the doors of God's Precious Ones or the Daughters of Hannah Shelter —
You inspired this story. You are proof that grace still wins. Thank you for trusting me to pour into you.

And finally, to my publisher and writing coach —
Thank you for hearing my voice, for refining my words, and for helping me bring this testimony to life with excellence. This wouldn't be what it is without you.

Introduction

Hey there, sis.

Before you turn another page, let me say this: **Thank you.**
Thank you for picking up this book. Thank you for leaning in. Thank you for being open enough to hear my story — the good, the bad, the holy, and the messy.

My name is Jeanette, and I've lived some life.
I've been the girl who felt invisible.

1

I've been the woman who gave too much
and got too little.
I've been the single mother crying into her
pillow at 3 a.m.
I've been the one who knew about the church,
but still ran from God.
I've been misunderstood, mislabeled,
misjudged and mistreated.

But I've also been **covered by grace.**
Over and over again, I've watched God
show up in my lowest moments and prove
that His hand was still on me even when I
didn't feel worthy of it.

This book isn't just a memoir.
It's a testimony.
It's a journey through fire and proof that you
can come out without smelling like smoke.

I didn't write this because I've done everything right. I wrote this because **God made everything right**, even after I messed it up. I wrote this for the woman who feels like she's too far gone, too dirty, too broken, or too tired to start over. Let me be the first to tell you — *you're not.*

If God could do it for me, He can do it for you.

So read this book slowly. Cry when you need to. Laugh when you can. Write on the pages I've provided for you. Talk back to the pages. Let God speak to you as He walks you through *my story*… and maybe begins to rewrite *your own.*

With love and truth,

Jeanette

CHAPTER 1

Covered Since Birth

I was born in Philadelphia, Pennsylvania, but raised in Harrisburg. I remember being five years old, so sick that my mama let me stay home from school. We didn't have much; my daddy didn't want my mother to work, but she had to anyway. We grew up on pork and beans and hot dogs — we ate that almost five days a week. Eight kids in a three-bedroom house, you couldn't pay me to eat baked beans and hot dogs today!

I think about the day my brother and I were so hungry that we climbed a small step ladder, trying to grab those hot dogs out of the pot. I couldn't have been more than six, and my brother was eight. When that boiling water poured out, it burned the left side of my arm and leg. My skin healed over the years, the scars blending into my complexion, but look close enough, and you'll see the reminder of what we survived.

That day, Mama had to leave me home with my daddy. I remember him lying in his bed, asking me to rub his back. I was only five, but I felt something strange when he asked, "Does it feel good sitting on Daddy's back?" Something in me said, *No.* I jumped off, ran outside into the bright, cold snow, and didn't look back.

At that moment, even at five, I knew there was something different about me. And let me be clear: my father never touched me inappropriately. He didn't harm me. In fact, I believe the Lord put him into a deep sleep that day to protect me. When I looked back, Daddy was knocked out, unaware I'd even left. *Hooray for me!* That's what I felt. *Hooray, Hooray, Hooray!*

I bundled up my coat, shoes, gloves, and hat, and hid under my neighbor's porch, shivering in the cold but wrapped in God's covering. Psalms 127 says, *"Children are an inheritance from the Lord, offspring a reward from him."* I didn't understand that at five, but now I see it clearly: God had my back even when I didn't know how to call on Him.

When Mama got home from work, she couldn't find me. She asked my daddy, whose name was James, "Where's Jeanette?" He didn't know. Without another word, Mama ran out into the snow yelling, *"Jeanette! Jeanette! Where are you?"* I was frozen and afraid, hiding under that porch, but I wasn't alone. Psalm 46:1 says, *"God is our refuge and strength, a very present help in trouble."*

So many times in life I've felt alone, but that verse is true: *"When my father and mother forsake me, then the Lord will take care of me"* (Psalm 27:10). Even back then, He was there. He's been there all along.

CHAPTER 2

When Rebellion Met Grace

I was brought up in a strict church, no pants, no makeup, no dancing. I told myself when I turned eighteen, I was moving out of my mama's house. She said, *"So be it! Jeanette, when you turn eighteen, I want you out."* I said to myself, *"Solid."*

I was rebellious. By sixteen, I was sneaking into clubs, acting twenty-one. Some folks said I was an old soul, but most just called me "that fast little girl." I was always the youngest in the crowd. I remember one night, out partying with my older girlfriends, my mama locked me out. Yes, she did! I had to climb through the basement window to get in. The next morning, she said, *"Next time, I'm locking those basement windows too!"* I just shrugged and thought, *"Next time, I'll be on my own."* I thank God she didn't hear me; she would've smacked the wind out of me!

I gave my life to the Lord at sixteen, but I didn't fully surrender. I kept running from His call, trying to do my own thing. But that same year, my whole world turned upside down. I became a statistic: a teenage pregnancy that everybody in town knew about. I was so ashamed. I felt like I had let my mother down. Sixteen years old, and I thought I was in love, swearing I'd marry this man. What did I know about love? I barely knew how to finish high school!

I skipped so much school; I prayed for a D in history just so I could graduate. And while I was supposed to be focused on my books, I was planning a future with a man way older than me. *What!*

But before I could even walk across that stage, tragedy hit. I went into labor at thirty-four weeks. The doctor told me my baby was gone. *"The fetus is dead,"* he said. I shouted, *"No! I feel him moving!"* But they said the movement was just the baby flopping inside me. I rode the bus home alone, tears rolling down my face, my mind in a daze.

When I got home, the hardest part was seeing all the baby things my mama had bought, that white bassinet in the dining room, dressed up with tiny clothes. She'd prepared a place for my baby boy, and now I had to tell her and his father's family that he was gone.

The doctor said my body had more white blood cells than red, and I was dangerously anemic. But none of that made it easier. I gave birth to a beautiful, full-sized baby boy. I named him Danielle. Dark-skinned, black hair, perfect. And yet, he never took a breath. I was seventeen, nearly eighteen, and fell into a deep depression. I wanted to end it all, to take every pill they'd given me to recover.

But I cried out to my mother. *"Baby girl,"* she said, *"what do you need me to do?"* I told her I wanted to leave Harrisburg and go to Atlanta to stay with family. She agreed. But what I didn't know was that the house I ended up in was a drug den, heroin needles, addicts all around. For two weeks, I watched family members shoot up in front of me. It was more than a teenage girl should ever see. All I could think was, *"I have to get out of here."*

I called my mama, *"Please send for me!"* That experience pulled me up out of that pit. I refused to let drugs swallow me like they did them. Psalm 34:18 says, *"The Lord is near to the brokenhearted and saves those who are crushed in spirit."* He did that for me.

Every last one of those family members died from that lifestyle. I didn't want them to die, but God warns us. *"He that diligently seeks good procures favor: but he that seeks mischief, it shall come unto him."* (Proverbs 11:27). Trouble chased them down, but grace chased me down, too.

CHAPTER 3

Not Too Far From Home

A t 18 years old, I finally moved out of my mama's house. But I didn't go far, just two blocks up the street. You know how we do… we want to be grown, but we still want to stay close enough to wash clothes and get a hot plate.

Every Saturday, I showed up at Mama's house with one big bag of laundry slung over my shoulder like I was headed to the laundromat. She'd see me coming from down the block, shake her head, and say, *"Only my daughter…"* I'd grin and head straight to the basement to wash my clothes and maybe grab a snack or two while I was at it.

Visiting Mama's house also meant crossing paths with Mr. Buster. Now, *Mr. Buster* Lord, have mercy, was an older man my mom took care of for years. He was an alcoholic, and when he drank, you could smell him a mile away.

He had a mean streak when he was drunk. He'd wave his arms and slur, *"I'm tired of y'all bad kids coming here shopping for food! This ain't no grocery store! You no good n——s!"* And I would just laugh, because he was stumbling back and forth, drunk and grumbling like clockwork.

But when Mr. Buster was sober, he was gentle. He'd cry and apologize, saying he didn't mean what he said. Still, when he was drinking, he could be dangerous. One day, I was stooping under the kitchen sink to grab some potatoes, where Mama kept them, and out of nowhere, he came up behind me and hit me in the head with a cast-iron frying pan. I saw stars.

I called my mama, tears streaming. She gasped, *"Oh my God, Jeanette, I'm so sorry!"* Then she said, *"Put him on the phone."* He got on, sobbing into the receiver, *"Herron, I'm sick of these kids coming in here taking all the food! You've worked too hard for this."*

I looked him dead in the eye and said, *"You better thank God you're drunk."*

Even in all that chaos, I kept running not just from danger, but from the Lord. But at 20 years old, I realized something: I could run, but I couldn't hide. There was **nowhere I could go that God couldn't reach me.**

CHAPTER 4

Running, Hiding, and Still Found by God

After I moved out of Mama's house, I started chasing what I thought was adulthood. I didn't know that running from home would turn into running from myself… and from God.

I bounced from place to place: Coatesville, Pennsylvania; Baton Rouge, Louisiana; Jacksonville, Florida; Atlanta, Georgia; and even the YMCA. Yep, I once lived in a

YMCA. Talk about trying to "find yourself" in all the wrong places. But God kept tracking me. No matter how far I ran, His mercy was still on my trail.

It was in Baton Rouge where my story got tangled up again, with a man. His name? Let's just call him *Russell*. Have you ever had a *Russell* in your life? Baby, I was on cloud 59. I was 20, and in my eyes, he was the best thing God ever made. He was my *boom-boom*. You couldn't tell me anything.

If he said, "Meet me," I said, "Where?" If he asked, "Wear this," I asked, "What color?"
Whatever Russell wanted, I gave.

But eventually, the truth came out. I wasn't his only one. I was the side chick, and I didn't even know it. That crushed me.

At the time, I was so focused on *why he hurt me* that I never stopped to ask *why I kept hurting myself.* I kept choosing men who didn't choose me back, and I didn't know my worth enough to stop it.

Heartbroken and soul-searching, I started hanging around a group of women I call my *sister-friends.* They had gone through some things, too. They were fighters, just like me, and being around them reminded me of home, of the big family I missed.

They invited me to Jimmy Swaggart's Singles Ministry one Sunday, but I refused. *"I'm not going to church,"* I told them. *"I'm going to Ladies' Night.* They rolled their eyes and said, *"Girl, you haven't been to church since you got here."* They weren't wrong.

I didn't want to be a hypocrite. I didn't want to be a liar. I was running from God, not to Him. After everything I'd been through, I didn't think God wanted me anymore. I thought, *"I'm damaged. Who would want me now?"*

But God wasn't finished with me.

One day, I finally agreed to visit a Holiness church. Whew! The moment I walked through the doors, I felt the power of God hit me like a wave. It was electrifying, like something deep inside me had woken up again. That visit stirred the fire I thought I'd lost. It reminded me of who I really was. *Not just Jeanette, the wanderer. Not just the heartbroken girl.* But Jeanette, the daughter of the Most High God.

CHAPTER 5

The Club, the Contest, and the Consequence

At that time in my life, I was desperate for a job… and maybe a little bit of attention too. I was in my early 20s, staying with one of my sister's friends, bouncing between uncertainty and survival. One day, while scrolling through radio stations, I heard an ad that said:

"Bikini contest — Friday night. $50 for the winner!"

And baby, that $50 sounded like a blessing. I said, *"I can do this."*

I still had my yellow bikini, size 8. And let me tell you, I was looking fine. A real brick house, as they used to say. I had gone to Barbizon Modeling School back in the day, and something about this contest brought that old confidence back.

My sister-friend raised her eyebrow and asked, *"You really doing this?"* I said, *"Why not?"*

So, we went. It was held at a club, of course. I wasn't saved at that moment; I was still in the world, still running from the call on my life. But that night? I was all in.

That's when I met him, the man who would become my baby daddy. I didn't know it then, and neither did he. But he was there that night, voting for me ten times. Yes, ten. And yes, I won.

Before the contest, I had joked, *"If I win, I'll take him out to breakfast."* So when the club closed, that's exactly what we did. We talked all night over pancakes and coffee, just vibing. He was sweet. Gentle. No pressure. Just good company.

After that, we started hanging out more as friends. He'd drive me around, wait for me after my waitress shifts, and make sure I got home safely. One night, I saw him standing in a club parking lot as the place emptied out. I said, *"What are you still doing here?"* He said, *"Making sure you get home safe."*

That melted my heart.

We were never in a relationship, just friends, but I was growing to appreciate how he looked out for me. Still, because of everything I'd been through with men before, I kept a wall up. I didn't want to be vulnerable again. I didn't want love, I wanted relief.

Then came my birthday party.

I invited a few friends over to my townhouse. I wasn't a drinker, but my girlfriends brought wine coolers. I had two bottles and got a little tipsy. One guy, a friend from out of town, asked to lie down before the party started. I said, *"Sure, no problem."* But then I realized my *baby daddy friend* was coming over. I told my girls, *"We need to wake him up and send him home. Things might happen tonight."*

And they did.

We partied, we laughed, and when everyone left, he stayed behind to help me clean up. Dishes. Vacuuming. Bathrooms. We were just talking… until one thing led to another.

The next morning, I looked at him and said, *"I'm pregnant."* He blinked and said, *"How can you know that in one night?"* I said, *"I feel it. I know I am."*

Two weeks later, I went to the doctor, and I was right. I was pregnant.

I panicked. Not because of him, he was happy, even asked, *"Is it mine?"* (Of course it was.) No, I panicked because I was raised in a strict, holiness church. No makeup. No short sleeves. No pants. No pregnancy outside of marriage.

I thought I was going to hell.

I dropped to my knees and cried, *"God, please forgive me. Please let my baby be healthy."*

I couldn't even tell my mama at first. I was so afraid she'd be ashamed. But she was a protector. The kind of mother who would say, *"My child didn't do it,"* even when she knew good and well I did.

Eventually, I told her, and do you know what she said?

"Come on back home, Jeanette."

I packed up my bags and returned to Harrisburg to have my son.

CHAPTER 6

From Shame to Single Motherhood

Nine months after that unforgettable birthday night, I gave birth to my son — Quincy Jermaine Long.

I was back in Harrisburg, living with my mother, just trying to figure things out. I had vowed I'd never return, but there I was. Back where it started, with a baby in my arms and a whole lot of fear in my heart.

After Quincy was born, I went back to Baton Rouge briefly, not to stay, but to give his father had the chance to meet his son. Then I moved again, this time to Jacksonville, Florida, to live with my sister Linda, who's now passed on. God rest her soul.

In Jacksonville, I got on welfare so I could have medical coverage for the baby. I took a job at a Publix grocery store and eventually got my own apartment. But I still wasn't walking with God. I knew I needed Him, but I wasn't ready to surrender.

Eventually, I started going to church again, the Church of God in Christ. I knew as soon as I stepped through those doors, the Holy Ghost was going to meet me at the entrance. And He did.

But life in Jacksonville was hard. The money was tight, and the pressure was heavy. I was doing everything in my power to avoid running back home again. But sometimes your power isn't enough; you need God's grace.

I bounced from one temporary job to another. I bartended at night, prayed during the day. There were moments I didn't know where my next meal would come from. Still, God covered me. Even when I didn't acknowledge Him fully, He never left me.

I remember sitting in my car, crying, praying, asking God to make a way. Looking back, I see how so many of those struggles could've been avoided if I had just surrendered, if I had just trusted Him from the beginning.

But that's what He does. He lets you live out your choices, and yet, He never stops extending His hand.

Eventually, I returned to Harrisburg again, for good this time, to raise my son. I started working with Manpower, a temp agency, and through them, I learned data entry, typing, and clerical work. They placed me with a computer company that handled medical claims, and it was there that my next season started to unfold.

That job taught me the skills I needed to elevate, and I didn't even realize it at the time. What I thought was just a job was really training for destiny.

And it all started while I was raising a baby on my own.

Motherhood matured me in ways nothing else ever could. It stretched me, broke me, and humbled me, but it also gave me purpose. I no longer lived just for me. Every diaper, every late-night feeding, every tear I wiped from Quincy's face reminded me: *I'm not doing this alone. God is still with me.*

I didn't have it all together. I was still learning how to trust God. Still learning how to let go of shame. Still learning how to be whole. But I was showing up every day for my son.

And somehow, even in my brokenness, God was building something beautiful.

CHAPTER 7

A Mother's Fight

Being a single mom wasn't just hard; it was war.

I was back in Harrisburg, trying to hold it all together for my son, Quincy. I worked at Capital Blue Shield and had to take all the overtime I could get just to make ends meet. That meant long hours, late nights, and sometimes asking the school to keep Quincy a little longer until I could pick him up.

But not everyone understood the life of a single mother.

One day, I got off work just an hour later than usual and found out that the school had put my five-year-old son outside to wait. Alone.

I couldn't believe it.

The building was still open, the school was still operating, but they made my baby sit outside because I was late.

Outside!
At five years old!

I was furious. I stormed into that school office like a mama bear on fire. The principal stood behind the counter with a blank expression, and I wanted to knock every emotion out of her face. The secretary looked at me like, *"Go ahead, sis. I don't even like her either."*

I told that woman, *"Don't you ever, and I mean ever, put my child outside by himself again! I work hard, I pay taxes, and you have a job because people like me show up every day!"*

I was shaking with rage. If I wasn't saved (or half-saved), it would've been a different kind of meeting. I might've had to lay hands, and not in the spiritual way.

That day, I learned that some people only see the stereotype. In her eyes, I was just another single Black mom. No husband. No father. No respect. But I wasn't just *anybody*; I was Quincy's mother. And I didn't play when it came to my son.

There was another time, years later, when Quincy had grown into a big young man.

He'd gone from small and quiet to strong and tall almost overnight. He loved football, and I encouraged him to play. I always told him, *"You're a star — go out there and shine."*

But one afternoon, after practice, a group of white boys jumped him. The school didn't say much until a teacher saw it happen. That teacher called the police and reported it.

Later that night, an officer came to our home to speak to Quincy. I had every right to press charges, but instead, I told them, *"What these boys need is counseling, not prison."*

Because that's the kind of mother I am. I'll fight for justice, but I'll also fight for healing. Even when the system is unjust, I refuse to let hate grow roots in my heart.

But I wasn't always calm. One time, I was driving home from Lancaster Bible College at night, and I saw police lights flashing off to the side of the road. I almost didn't look; I was used to cops pulling over young Black men for nothing.

But something told me to look again. *That's my son.*

I slammed on the brakes and pulled over without even checking for cars behind me. Walked a half-mile back up the road to where they had him stopped. The officer said, *"Oh, you called your mother?"*

Quincy said, *"No, God did."*

Whew! That did something to me.

I told those officers, *"What's going on here?"* and I didn't care what they thought. I wasn't just a mom, I was a prayer warrior with keys to the kingdom. And if they touched my son, they were gonna meet both me and the Lord that night.

It turns out they were giving him a speeding ticket and had taken his motorcycle. They had no plan for how he'd get home. But God did. He sent me, and I showed up.

I'm not ashamed to say I'm one of those mamas who will go down to the football field and fight the coach if he doesn't play my son. Call me what you want, but you better respect me when it comes to my child.

All that to say: I know what it means to raise a son alone. I know what it means to be judged, misunderstood, and overlooked. And that's why my heart will always be with other single mothers.

I've been in their shoes.

And I'm still standing.

CHAPTER 8

Favor in the Wilderness

After everything I'd been through, the heartbreak, the moves, the jobs, the struggles, I was still standing. But not just standing… I was walking in favor, and I didn't even know it.

When I moved back to Harrisburg for good, I didn't have a plan. I just knew I had a child to raise and a God who wouldn't let me fall. Manpower, a local temp agency, became my lifeline. They placed me in job after job, and every assignment taught me something new.

Data entry. Clerical work. Medical forms. Customer service. Whatever they sent me to do, I did it with everything I had.

One of my assignments was with a small computer company. To my surprise, they were using the same medical billing software I had worked with in Baton Rouge. *Only God could've lined that up.* I went in as a temporary employee, but I ended up being the one teaching them how to use the system.

It wasn't paying much, not enough to make ends meet, but it was enough for me to gain confidence. I kept hearing a small voice say, *"Apply at Blue Shield."*
At first, I ignored it.
"I'm not qualified."

"I don't have a degree."

"That's for people with experience."

But the voice didn't stop. One day, during my lunch break, I walked into Capital Blue Cross and Blue Shield, filled out the application, and took the entrance test.

It was for a data entry position.

I aced it.

I was hired.

And just like that, God planted me in a stable job that gave me a steady income, medical benefits, and the space I needed to breathe. I was making $24,000 a year, and coming from minimum wage, that felt like *big money.* You couldn't tell me I wasn't on top of the world! (I was making boo-coo money, honey!)

That job changed everything.

It gave me the ability to buy my first home. It allowed me to raise Quincy in a stable environment.
It introduced me to skills, coworkers, and systems that would later help me build my business.

But it wasn't all easy.

My first position at Blue Shield came with strict quotas. I had to process a certain number of claims per day, and if I didn't meet the numbers, I felt like I was failing. I'd go home crying sometimes, overwhelmed and exhausted. But I kept pushing. I worked overtime, stayed late, and did whatever it took to keep that job.

Eventually, I applied for a new position within the company and landed a role in third-party administration. No quotas. No performance tracking. Just honest work. And I loved it.

I found my rhythm. I found my peace. But change was coming.

Blue Cross and Blue Shield were in the middle of a major split, the company was downsizing, rebranding, and shifting into what would eventually become **Highmark**. Nobody knew who would be let go. Whispers of layoffs floated through the hallways like cold wind.

So, I started preparing.

I prayed. I wrote down my dreams. I asked God to show me what was next.

And one day, walking down the street, I passed an early learning center. My heart lit up.

"Lord," I whispered, *"I would love to have a daycare center like that. I want to create a space for children. I want to help mothers like me, women who are trying to raise kids and still survive."*

God heard me.

Not my shout.

Not a Facebook post.

Not a church testimony.

Just a quiet prayer in my heart.

He heard me.

And when I finally got laid off from Blue Shield, I panicked at first. I couldn't breathe. Literally. I had an anxiety attack in the parking lot. But I heard the Lord say, **"Breathe, Jeanette. Just breathe."**

When I got home and collected myself, I called my mama.

"Mama, I got laid off."

She didn't even flinch.

"Then it's time," she said. *"Go full-time with your business. God is making a way."*

At first, I couldn't receive it. I was too caught up in the shock of what I lost to recognize what I'd just gained.

But then the checks came in:

My pension.

My 401(k).My severance package.

I had over $60,000 in hand, more than I'd ever seen in my life at one time.

And all I could do was laugh.

"God, you really did it… didn't you?"

CHAPTER 9

When God Says, "Start the Dream"

After the layoff from Blue Shield, I thought everything was falling apart, but God was actually setting everything in motion. What felt like a loss was really the launchpad. The prayers I whispered in the hallways and on my lunch breaks were now becoming a reality.

With the severance and savings I received, I did something bold:
I started my business.

At first, it was small, just babysitting in my apartment. I didn't have a staff. I didn't have fancy equipment. I didn't even have extra space. But what I *did* have was love for children, a heart for single mothers, and a calling from God.

Before long, the kids filled the room. The word spread fast:

"Miss Jeanette is good with the babies!"

Soon, my little apartment couldn't hold it anymore. I transitioned to the home I bought through Blue Shield and remodeled the basement into a daycare space. We hung up posters, painted walls, and filled the shelves with books and toys. I may not have had the biggest center yet, but it was *mine*. And it was *God-breathed.*

That center was called **God's Little Angels.**

From that humble beginning, God expanded me.

What started with a few kids in my apartment grew into **three full centers.** Yes — *three.*
I asked God to increase my territory, and He did just that. I didn't even know how I was going to manage it all… but He gave me wisdom, workers, and resources.

Eventually, I merged all three locations into one large center that could serve more families, a building big enough to house every vision God gave me. The name became **God's Precious Ones, Inc.,** and it still stands as a testimony to what happens when you trust Him.

But I didn't stop there.

I went back to school and earned my Associate Degree in Human Services. Then I kept going and graduated from Lancaster Bible College with my **Bachelor's in Ministry**.

Yes, the girl who barely passed history class, the one who got pregnant at 16, the one who ran from God, *that* girl walked across the stage with a degree in her hand and purpose in her heart.

God was doing it. And he was doing it big.

All of it, the education, the centers, the staff, the space, was for one main purpose: **to help people, especially single mothers.** I had lived their story. I had worn their shoes. I knew what it felt like to feel like no one saw you, no one understood, and no one cared.

That's why I poured myself into it, because I was raising Quincy while building all of this. I was navigating parent-teacher meetings, doctor visits, and groceries with one hand while submitting license forms and organizing payroll with the other. But I did it. With God, I did it.

CHAPTER 10

The Birth of the Daughters of Hannah Shelter

If raising Quincy gave me strength… and launching my centers gave me purpose… then **birthing the Daughters of Hannah Shelter** gave me a legacy.

This dream didn't come overnight. It grew in me slowly, through every broken moment, every prayer in the dark, every time I watched a struggling mother walk through my center doors and try her best to hold it all together.

I saw myself in them, in their tired eyes, their quiet desperation, their bold determination.

That's when I knew:
This is more than daycare. This is ministry.

The dream to create a shelter didn't start with paperwork; it started with people. Real people. Real women. Women who had nowhere to go. Women who were couch-hopping with children in tow. Women who didn't need a handout, but a chance to breathe.

And I had an empty house.

Years ago, I bought a second home. Initially, I used it as a rental property, sometimes renting it out on Section 8 to help low-income families, and at other times, I utilized it for extra income. But the taxes started climbing. I owed over $20,000, and it was getting hard to keep up.

So, I prayed.

And the Lord spoke:
"Use what's in your hand."

So, I did. I opened that house as a shelter for women and children, a safe space for single mothers who had nowhere else to go. It wasn't fancy, but it was clean. It was warm. And it was filled with love.

I didn't know it yet, but that was the **birthing room** for what would later become the **"Daughters of Hannah Shelter."**

Why Hannah? Because Hannah knew what it meant to cry from the depths of her soul. She knew what it meant to long for something more. And when God finally answered her cry, she dedicated the blessing right back to Him.

That's how I felt.

I had cried. I had waited. I had been misunderstood. And now, I was giving birth, not to a baby, but to a movement.

The Daughters of Hannah Shelter became a **501(c)(3) nonprofit**, and I made it my mission to provide more than just a roof. I wanted to give women hope, direction, spiritual encouragement, life skills, and the tools to rise again.

I started looking for the perfect building — a space that could house women with dignity and provide real services, not just temporary relief. I wasn't building a shelter... I was building a *refuge.*

I believed, and still believe, that God will guide my steps to the right property, the right grants, the right partnerships. Because this work isn't mine. It's His. I'm just the vessel.

And listen, I know not every woman who walked through my door came with good intentions. Some were users. Some tried to manipulate, to scheme, to take advantage of kindness.

But the Lord reminded me:

"You're not responsible for their heart. You're responsible for your obedience."

And sometimes, even the users got healed not because of anything I did, but because they encountered **unearned grace.**

That's what the Daughters of Hannah Shelter is about.

It's not just a program. It's not just transitional housing.
It's a divine response to a desperate need.

And I'm just honored that God chose me.

CHAPTER 11

Pearls of Purpose

I've come to realize something deeply sacred about single mothers:

They are **God's pearls.**

Why pearls? Because pearls are born in darkness. They're formed through irritation, through pressure, through hidden struggle, and yet, they emerge whole. Beautiful. Rare. Priceless.

And isn't that what single mothers are?

We carry so much: the weight of our children, the judgment of society, the pressure to hold everything together. We stretch every dollar, work multiple jobs, wipe tears, kiss boo-boos, and fight for our babies, all while trying to heal ourselves.

That's why I say:

Single mothers are not broken.

They are battle-tested.

They are not less-than.

They are Heaven's chosen.

They are not victims.

They are pearls of great price.

Matthew 13:45–46 says, *"Again, the kingdom of heaven is like a merchant looking for fine pearls. When he found one of great value, he went away and sold everything he had and bought it."*

That verse doesn't just describe treasure —
it describes *worth.*

And single moms? You are worth it.

You're worth the time.

You're worth the investment.

You're worth the love.

You're worth the grace.

That's why I fight so hard for them, because
I *am* one.

I've lived the shame.

I've cried the tears.

I've prayed over empty refrigerators.

I've shown up to parent-teacher meetings in
scrubs, with a baby on one hip and
exhaustion in my bones.

And I've also watched God turn   *every
struggle* into strength.

That's what birthed **The Daughters of Hannah Shelter.**

That's what birthed **God's Precious Ones.**

That's what birthed my desire to **pour into single mothers, not just with resources, but with *recognition.***

You matter.

You carry the weight of nations.

You raise prophets, preachers, teachers, doctors, entrepreneurs — in your lap, while folding laundry, while crying in the bathroom between shifts.

And you are not forgotten.

I see you.

More importantly, **God sees you.**

I wrote this book not just to tell my story, but to remind every single mama that your story still matters. You are not invisible. You are not disposable. You are not finished.

You're just getting started.

Chapter Reflection Questions

Chapter 1: Covered Since Birth

- What early experiences in your childhood made you feel "set apart" or protected?

_____

_____

_____

_____

_____

_____

_____

_____

- Have you ever felt God shield you from harm, even when you didn't understand it at the time?

_____

_____

_____

_____

_____

_____

_____

_____

Chapter 2: Rebellion, Religion, and Reality

- What rules from your upbringing still impact the way you view yourself today?

_____

_____

_____

_____

_____

_____

_____

_____

- Have you ever confused rebellion with freedom? What did it cost you?

_____

_____

_____

_____

_____

_____

_____

_____

Chapter 3: Not Too Far From Home

- Was there a time when you tried to be grown, but still needed your mother?

_____

_____

_____

_____

_____

_____

_____

_____

- How do you now view the people who helped raise you, flaws and all?

_____

_____

_____

_____

_____

_____

_____

_____

Chapter 4: Running, Hiding, and Still Found by God

- What are the places you've tried to run to, thinking God wouldn't find you there?

_____

_____

_____

_____

_____

_____

_____

_____

- Have you ever felt unworthy of God's love? What does His pursuit of you say about His character?

_____

_____

_____

_____

_____

_____

_____

_____

Chapter 5: The Club, the Contest, and the Consequence

• Can you recall a time when you felt seen… but not truly valued?

_____

_____

_____

_____

_____

_____

_____

_____

• How did one decision change the course of your life?

_____

_____

_____

_____

_____

_____

_____

_____

Chapter 6: From Shame to Single Motherhood

- What did becoming a mother awaken in you, fear, strength, or both?

_____

_____

_____

_____

_____

_____

_____

_____

- How did motherhood change the way you viewed yourself?

_____

_____

_____

_____

_____

_____

_____

_____

Chapter 7: A Mother's Fight

• Have you ever had to fight for your child to be seen, safe, or supported?

_____

_____

_____

_____

_____

_____

_____

_____

• What would you say to your younger "mama self" if you could encourage her today?

_____

_____

_____

_____

_____

_____

_____

_____

Chapter 8: Favor in the Wilderness

- Have you ever been blessed and still afraid?

_____

_____

_____

_____

_____

_____

_____

_____

- How has God provided for you in ways that didn't make sense at the time?

_____

_____

_____

_____

_____

_____

_____

_____

Chapter 9: When God Says, "Start the Dream

• What dream has been sitting quietly in your heart, waiting on your "yes"?

_____

_____

_____

_____

_____

_____

_____

_____

• How do you handle fear when God calls you to start something new?

_____

_____

_____

_____

_____

_____

_____

_____

Chapter 10: The Birth of the Daughters of Hannah Shelter

- Who are you called to serve, based on the life you've lived?

_____

_____

_____

_____

_____

_____

_____

_____

- Are you willing to go from survival to service and let God use your story?

_____

_____

_____

_____

_____

_____

_____

_____

Chapter 11: Pearls of Purpose

• In what ways are you like a pearl, shaped by pain, but priceless in purpose?

_____

_____

_____

_____

_____

_____

_____

_____

• What does it mean to you to be God's chosen, even with your flaws?

_____

_____

_____

_____

_____

_____

_____

_____

ABOUT THE AUTHOR

 **Jeanette Long** is a devoted servant of God whose life has been marked by unwavering faith, perseverance, and a heart for people. Called by God at just 16 years old, she embraced her divine assignment early and has spent decades walking faithfully in ministry.

She earned her Associate's Degree in Human Services from Harrisburg Area Community College (HAAC) and later obtained her Bachelor's Degree in Ministry from Lancaster Bible College, equipping her with both spiritual insight and practical skills to serve her community.

Jeanette is the visionary founder of **Grace Outreach Destiny Church International**, **God's Precious Ones Early Learning Center**, and **Daughters of Hannah's Orphanage**, ministries and organizations dedicated to spiritual growth, education, and the care of God's children, both locally and abroad.

Her ministry journey began under the late Apostle Carl E. Hines Jr. of the Church of God in Christ, where she faithfully served for over 20 years. Under his mentorship, she developed a strong biblical foundation and a servant's heart. In obedience to God's direction, she later stepped into a new season, assisting other pastors and ministries, before being ordained as a Pastor under the leadership of phenomenal Bishop Norman Brown Jr.

Apostle Jeanette Long is an active member of the Global Media Ministries, Restoration Multimedia Ministries, and Restoration Fellowship of Churches under the leadership of Chief Apostle/Bishop Michael Jones.

Today, Apostle Jeanette Long continues to lead **Grace Outreach Destiny Church International** in Harrisburg, Pennsylvania, where she has served as Senior Apostle for the past three years. Her passion is to see lives transformed by the power of God, to nurture leaders, and to create safe places for children and families to thrive.

With every message she preaches and every soul she serves, Apostle Long's life reflects her personal motto: *"It's not just ministry—it's destiny."*